WRITE-IN JOURNAL

LIVING WITH GRATITUDE

*Count Your Blessings, Connect With
Your Heart, and Nurture Your Soul*

DARA KURTZ

AUTHOR OF I AM MY MOTHER'S DAUGHTER

crazy perfect life

Copyright © 2023. Dara Kurtz.
All rights reserved.

ISBN: 978-0-9988404-2-0

Produced by Publish Pros | www.publishpros.com

GRATITUDE MATTERS

I wasn't always someone who counted my blessings instead of my problems. Living with gratitude was something I had to learn and practice before it became a habit. I'm a lot happier and more joyful since I've incorporated a daily gratitude practice in my life, and you can be too.

I've been using a gratitude journal to help start my day in a positive manner for a long time. After I write down what I'm grateful for, I take a few moments to also write about what's going on in my life. This isn't a daily to-do list, just how I'm feeling about whatever is going on in my life. Journaling helps me work out challenges, learn things about myself, and gain insight about my life.

For a long time, I wanted to create a gratitude journal that incorporated all of this, a one-stop shop to help others think about this quickly and impactfully. I wanted a way for them to connect with their heart, nurture their soul, and find a way to feel as good as possible each day. That's where self-care comes in. Self-care is such a buzzword these days, but to me, it's the action we take to show we love ourselves. It doesn't take a lot of time or cost a lot of money to intentionally find a way to incorporate self-care into your day, as you will see in the examples below. What it will do is help you feel your best!

This daily gratitude journal is designed to help you train your mind to find the blessings in your life—even the small ones. Studies show that cultivating an attitude of gratitude can have a number of positive benefits, including increased happiness and well-being, improved relationships, and better physical health. It's also free, doesn't take a lot of time, and is available to everyone.

Living with gratitude is about being grateful for all the good in your life, even when it's not perfect. Learning to find the good, even when you don't like something you're dealing with, will help you navigate life's challenges with more ease and grace. This doesn't mean subscribing to toxic positivity or not allowing yourself to feel all of your emotions. Of course you aren't going to feel grateful all the time, and that's OK. Counting your blessings and taking the time to see the positive in your life, even though life isn't perfect, will help you be the best version of yourself.

Use this journal to help you record what you're grateful for every day. Journal about how you're feeling and take time to nurture your soul. Write down any thoughts you might have about whatever is going on in your life and set your intention for the day. Think about how you want to feel, what you can do to help yourself feel the way you want to feel, and consider inserting a little dose of self care into your life. Doing this daily, preferably at the same time, will help you learn to look for the good, shift your mindset to being more positive, and feel happier and more joyful.

It's exciting to get to know yourself better and get more of what you want from your life, and I hope you enjoy using this journal. Feel free to contact me through my website at www.crazyperfectlife.com or on Instagram @crazyperflife or Facebook @crazyperfectlife.

So much love,

Dara

EASY SELF-CARE SUGGESTIONS:

Self-care actions don't have to be big or time-consuming to have a positive impact. By being intentional about inserting self-care into your daily life, you will ultimately feel happier and more joyful, and you will be helping yourself get more of what you want from your life. Here are some simple, effective ways to incorporate self-care into your day.

1. **Meditation:** Find a quiet and comfortable place to sit or lie down. Close your eyes and focus on your breath, letting go of any racing thoughts or distractions. Start with a few minutes and gradually increase the length of your meditation practice.

2. **Exercise:** Engage in physical activity you enjoy, such as going for a walk, run, or bike ride, or taking a yoga class. Aim for at least 30 minutes of moderate to vigorous exercise a day. If you don't have a lot of time, try to just move your body. Even taking a five minute walk outside can help you clear your mind.

3. **Journaling:** Take a few minutes each day to write down your thoughts and feelings. This can help you process your emotions and be a therapeutic outlet. This journal has a space designated for this called "Today I'm Thinking About..."

4. **Relaxation techniques:** Try deep breathing, progressive muscle relaxation, or guided imagery to relax and unwind.

5. **Time in nature:** Spend time outdoors in nature, whether it's a hike in the woods, a walk through a park, or sitting by the ocean. Even just sitting outside for fifteen minutes and feeling the sunshine on your face can help you feel happier. Being in nature has been shown to have a calming and rejuvenating effect.

6. **Eating well:** Pay attention to what you're putting in your body and how the food you eat makes you feel. Drink plenty of water, eat real food, and decrease your intake of processed food.

7. **Hobbies and creative pursuits:** Engage in activities that bring you joy and allow you to express your creativity, such as painting, drawing, knitting, or cooking.

8. **Connect with a close friend or family member:** Connecting and sharing with people who have your back is a great form of self-care. Even just a quick phone call or video chat can help you feel loved and less isolated.

9. **Alone time:** Spending time alone, whether it's reading an inspirational book, taking a warm bath, or drinking a hot cup of tea, can help you feel calmer and more grounded.

10. **Sleep:** Prioritize getting enough sleep by establishing a consistent bedtime routine and creating a sleep-friendly environment. Aim for 7-9 hours of sleep every night.

LIVING WITH GRATITUDE

*Count Your Blessings, Connect With
Your Heart, and Nurture Your Soul*

DARA KURTZ

"I'm moving forward. One day at a time, one step at a time. It might be hard, but I'm going to keep on keeping on."

TODAY, I AM GRATEFUL FOR:

1.

2.

3.

TODAY, I AM THINKING ABOUT:

LIVING WITH GRATITUDE

TODAY, I AM FEELING:

AN ACTION I CAN TAKE TODAY TO HELP ME FEEL THE WAY I WANT IS:

TODAY, I INTEND TO:

I AM PRACTICING SELF-CARE TODAY BY:

DARA KURTZ

*"I can spend my life worrying
or I can decide to live each day to the fullest.
My life, my choice."*

TODAY, I AM GRATEFUL FOR:

1.

2.

3.

TODAY, I AM THINKING ABOUT:

LIVING WITH GRATITUDE

TODAY, I AM FEELING:

AN ACTION I CAN TAKE TODAY TO HELP ME FEEL THE WAY I WANT IS:

TODAY, I INTEND TO:

I AM PRACTICING SELF-CARE TODAY BY:

DARA KURTZ

"Your future is whatever you have the courage to make it."

TODAY, I AM GRATEFUL FOR:

1.

2.

3.

TODAY, I AM THINKING ABOUT:

LIVING WITH GRATITUDE

TODAY, I AM FEELING:

AN ACTION I CAN TAKE TODAY TO HELP ME FEEL THE WAY I WANT IS:

TODAY, I INTEND TO:

I AM PRACTICING SELF-CARE TODAY BY:

"When you take the time to practice self care each day, you're showing yourself you matter."

TODAY, I AM GRATEFUL FOR:

1.

2.

3.

TODAY, I AM THINKING ABOUT:

LIVING WITH GRATITUDE

TODAY, I AM FEELING:

AN ACTION I CAN TAKE TODAY TO HELP ME FEEL THE WAY I WANT IS:

TODAY, I INTEND TO:

I AM PRACTICING SELF-CARE TODAY BY:

"Be the version of yourself you've been dreaming about, not who other people tell you to be."

TODAY, I AM GRATEFUL FOR:

1.

2.

3.

TODAY, I AM THINKING ABOUT:

LIVING WITH GRATITUDE

TODAY, I AM FEELING:

AN ACTION I CAN TAKE TODAY TO HELP ME FEEL THE WAY I WANT IS:

TODAY, I INTEND TO:

I AM PRACTICING SELF-CARE TODAY BY:

"The only person whose opinion truly matters is yours. If you think you can, you're right. If you think you can't, you're right. Tune out everyone else and tap into your soul."

TODAY, I AM GRATEFUL FOR:

1.

2.

3.

TODAY, I AM THINKING ABOUT:

LIVING WITH GRATITUDE

TODAY, I AM FEELING:

AN ACTION I CAN TAKE TODAY TO HELP ME FEEL THE WAY I WANT IS:

TODAY, I INTEND TO:

I AM PRACTICING SELF-CARE TODAY BY:

"Perfection doesn't exist. If you're striving for perfection, you're going to lose every time."

TODAY, I AM GRATEFUL FOR:

1.

2.

3.

TODAY, I AM THINKING ABOUT:

LIVING WITH GRATITUDE

TODAY, I AM FEELING:

AN ACTION I CAN TAKE TODAY TO HELP ME FEEL THE WAY I WANT IS:

TODAY, I INTEND TO:

I AM PRACTICING SELF-CARE TODAY BY:

> *"The hardest moments of your life are also the greatest opportunities to grow the most."*

TODAY, I AM GRATEFUL FOR:

1.

2.

3.

TODAY, I AM THINKING ABOUT:

LIVING WITH GRATITUDE

TODAY, I AM FEELING:

AN ACTION I CAN TAKE TODAY TO HELP ME FEEL THE WAY I WANT IS:

TODAY, I INTEND TO:

I AM PRACTICING SELF-CARE TODAY BY:

DARA KURTZ

*"Making mistakes is part of the game.
If you aren't making mistakes you aren't
taking enough risks."*

TODAY, I AM GRATEFUL FOR:

1.

2.

3.

TODAY, I AM THINKING ABOUT:

LIVING WITH GRATITUDE

TODAY, I AM FEELING:

AN ACTION I CAN TAKE TODAY TO HELP ME FEEL THE WAY I WANT IS:

TODAY, I INTEND TO:

I AM PRACTICING SELF-CARE TODAY BY:

"Life is made up of moments. It's what you do with these moments that determines everything."

TODAY, I AM GRATEFUL FOR:

1.

2.

3.

TODAY, I AM THINKING ABOUT:

LIVING WITH GRATITUDE

TODAY, I AM FEELING:

AN ACTION I CAN TAKE TODAY TO HELP ME FEEL THE WAY I WANT IS:

TODAY, I INTEND TO:

I AM PRACTICING SELF-CARE TODAY BY:

Time to Check In

HOW IS YOUR DAILY GRATITUDE PRACTICE GOING?

ARE YOU STAYING CONSISTENT? IF NOT, WHAT CAN YOU DO TO HELP YOURSELF RECOMMIT?

DO YOU FEEL GOOD ABOUT THE PROGRESS YOU'RE MAKING?

LIVING WITH GRATITUDE

WHAT ARE YOU LEARNING ABOUT YOURSELF?

HOW DO YOU FEEL ABOUT INCORPORATING DAILY SELF-CARE INTO YOUR LIFE?

WHAT DO YOU WANT MORE OF?

Stay committed and keep moving forward!

"All you have is today. Make peace with your past mistakes and stop trying to control the future."

TODAY, I AM GRATEFUL FOR:

1.

2.

3.

TODAY, I AM THINKING ABOUT:

LIVING WITH GRATITUDE

TODAY, I AM FEELING:

AN ACTION I CAN TAKE TODAY TO HELP ME FEEL THE WAY I WANT IS:

TODAY, I INTEND TO:

I AM PRACTICING SELF-CARE TODAY BY:

"Happiness is your human right. Be intentional about achieving it."

TODAY, I AM GRATEFUL FOR:

1.

2.

3.

TODAY, I AM THINKING ABOUT:

LIVING WITH GRATITUDE

TODAY, I AM FEELING:

AN ACTION I CAN TAKE TODAY TO HELP ME FEEL THE WAY I WANT IS:

TODAY, I INTEND TO:

I AM PRACTICING SELF-CARE TODAY BY:

"Figure out who your people are, then figure out how to spend time with them."

TODAY, I AM GRATEFUL FOR:

1.

2.

3.

TODAY, I AM THINKING ABOUT:

LIVING WITH GRATITUDE

TODAY, I AM FEELING:

AN ACTION I CAN TAKE TODAY TO HELP ME FEEL THE WAY I WANT IS:

TODAY, I INTEND TO:

I AM PRACTICING SELF-CARE TODAY BY:

*"A peaceful mind creates
a peaceful body."*

TODAY, I AM GRATEFUL FOR:

1.

2.

3.

TODAY, I AM THINKING ABOUT:

LIVING WITH GRATITUDE

TODAY, I AM FEELING:

AN ACTION I CAN TAKE TODAY TO HELP ME FEEL THE WAY I WANT IS:

TODAY, I INTEND TO:

I AM PRACTICING SELF-CARE TODAY BY:

"Your daily habits can get you where you want to go—or hold you back."

TODAY, I AM GRATEFUL FOR:

1.

2.

3.

TODAY, I AM THINKING ABOUT:

LIVING WITH GRATITUDE

TODAY, I AM FEELING:

AN ACTION I CAN TAKE TODAY TO HELP ME FEEL THE WAY I WANT IS:

TODAY, I INTEND TO:

I AM PRACTICING SELF-CARE TODAY BY:

"Happiness is a choice we make for ourselves every day."

TODAY, I AM GRATEFUL FOR:

1.

2.

3.

TODAY, I AM THINKING ABOUT:

LIVING WITH GRATITUDE

TODAY, I AM FEELING:

AN ACTION I CAN TAKE TODAY TO HELP ME FEEL THE WAY I WANT IS:

TODAY, I INTEND TO:

I AM PRACTICING SELF-CARE TODAY BY:

"Being content with your life and the choices you've made is a gift no one can take from you."

TODAY, I AM GRATEFUL FOR:

1.

2.

3.

TODAY, I AM THINKING ABOUT:

LIVING WITH GRATITUDE

TODAY, I AM FEELING:

AN ACTION I CAN TAKE TODAY TO HELP ME FEEL THE WAY I WANT IS:

TODAY, I INTEND TO:

I AM PRACTICING SELF-CARE TODAY BY:

"If you don't make yourself a priority, don't expect anyone else to either."

TODAY, I AM GRATEFUL FOR:

1.

2.

3.

TODAY, I AM THINKING ABOUT:

LIVING WITH GRATITUDE

TODAY, I AM FEELING:

AN ACTION I CAN TAKE TODAY TO HELP ME FEEL THE WAY I WANT IS:

TODAY, I INTEND TO:

I AM PRACTICING SELF-CARE TODAY BY:

"A grateful heart creates a joyful soul."

TODAY, I AM GRATEFUL FOR:

1.

2.

3.

TODAY, I AM THINKING ABOUT:

LIVING WITH GRATITUDE

TODAY, I AM FEELING:

AN ACTION I CAN TAKE TODAY TO HELP ME FEEL THE WAY I WANT IS:

TODAY, I INTEND TO:

I AM PRACTICING SELF-CARE TODAY BY:

DARA KURTZ

"Wake up and notice the blessings in your life every day. If you can't see them, keep looking. They're there."

TODAY, I AM GRATEFUL FOR:

1.

2.

3.

TODAY, I AM THINKING ABOUT:

LIVING WITH GRATITUDE

TODAY, I AM FEELING:

AN ACTION I CAN TAKE TODAY TO HELP ME FEEL THE WAY I WANT IS:

TODAY, I INTEND TO:

I AM PRACTICING SELF-CARE TODAY BY:

Time to Check In

HOW IS YOUR DAILY GRATITUDE PRACTICE GOING?

ARE YOU STAYING CONSISTENT? IF NOT, WHAT CAN YOU DO TO HELP YOURSELF RECOMMIT?

DO YOU FEEL GOOD ABOUT THE PROGRESS YOU'RE MAKING?

WHAT ARE YOU LEARNING ABOUT YOURSELF?

HOW DO YOU FEEL ABOUT INCORPORATING DAILY SELF-CARE INTO YOUR LIFE?

WHAT DO YOU WANT MORE OF?

Stay committed and keep moving forward!

"Get comfortable spending time alone. When you learn to be your own best friend, magical things can happen."

TODAY, I AM GRATEFUL FOR:

1.

2.

3.

TODAY, I AM THINKING ABOUT:

LIVING WITH GRATITUDE

TODAY, I AM FEELING:

AN ACTION I CAN TAKE TODAY TO HELP ME FEEL THE WAY I WANT IS:

TODAY, I INTEND TO:

I AM PRACTICING SELF-CARE TODAY BY:

"Creating a meaningful life takes work, but it's one of the most important jobs of your life."

TODAY, I AM GRATEFUL FOR:

1.

2.

3.

TODAY, I AM THINKING ABOUT:

LIVING WITH GRATITUDE

TODAY, I AM FEELING:

AN ACTION I CAN TAKE TODAY TO HELP ME FEEL THE WAY I WANT IS:

TODAY, I INTEND TO:

I AM PRACTICING SELF-CARE TODAY BY:

"Stop listening to other people; listen to the voice inside yourself."

TODAY, I AM GRATEFUL FOR:

1.

2.

3.

TODAY, I AM THINKING ABOUT:

LIVING WITH GRATITUDE

TODAY, I AM FEELING:

AN ACTION I CAN TAKE TODAY TO HELP ME FEEL THE WAY I WANT IS:

TODAY, I INTEND TO:

I AM PRACTICING SELF-CARE TODAY BY:

*"You will never figure out the answers
if you never ask the questions."*

TODAY, I AM GRATEFUL FOR:

1.

2.

3.

TODAY, I AM THINKING ABOUT:

LIVING WITH GRATITUDE

TODAY, I AM FEELING:

AN ACTION I CAN TAKE TODAY TO HELP ME FEEL THE WAY I WANT IS:

TODAY, I INTEND TO:

I AM PRACTICING SELF-CARE TODAY BY:

"Failure is part of life. When something doesn't go the way you want, learn from it and try again."

TODAY, I AM GRATEFUL FOR:

1.

2.

3.

TODAY, I AM THINKING ABOUT:

LIVING WITH GRATITUDE

TODAY, I AM FEELING:

AN ACTION I CAN TAKE TODAY TO HELP ME FEEL THE WAY I WANT IS:

TODAY, I INTEND TO:

I AM PRACTICING SELF-CARE TODAY BY:

DARA KURTZ

"You don't have to have everything figured out. Just start, and the rest will follow."

TODAY, I AM GRATEFUL FOR:

1.

2.

3.

TODAY, I AM THINKING ABOUT:

LIVING WITH GRATITUDE

TODAY, I AM FEELING:

AN ACTION I CAN TAKE TODAY TO HELP ME FEEL THE WAY I WANT IS:

TODAY, I INTEND TO:

I AM PRACTICING SELF-CARE TODAY BY:

"Getting to know yourself is the greatest gift."

TODAY, I AM GRATEFUL FOR:

1.

2.

3.

TODAY, I AM THINKING ABOUT:

LIVING WITH GRATITUDE

TODAY, I AM FEELING:

AN ACTION I CAN TAKE TODAY TO HELP ME FEEL THE WAY I WANT IS:

TODAY, I INTEND TO:

I AM PRACTICING SELF-CARE TODAY BY:

"Trust the Universe is on your side and that all you want is on its way to you."

TODAY, I AM GRATEFUL FOR:

1.

2.

3.

TODAY, I AM THINKING ABOUT:

LIVING WITH GRATITUDE

TODAY, I AM FEELING:

AN ACTION I CAN TAKE TODAY TO HELP ME FEEL THE WAY I WANT IS:

TODAY, I INTEND TO:

I AM PRACTICING SELF-CARE TODAY BY:

> *"Counting your blessings is the secret to a happy life."*

TODAY, I AM GRATEFUL FOR:

1.

2.

3.

TODAY, I AM THINKING ABOUT:

LIVING WITH GRATITUDE

TODAY, I AM FEELING:

AN ACTION I CAN TAKE TODAY TO HELP ME FEEL THE WAY I WANT IS:

TODAY, I INTEND TO:

I AM PRACTICING SELF-CARE TODAY BY:

*"Focus on what you have,
not what you lack."*

TODAY, I AM GRATEFUL FOR:

1.

2.

3.

TODAY, I AM THINKING ABOUT:

LIVING WITH GRATITUDE

TODAY, I AM FEELING:

AN ACTION I CAN TAKE TODAY TO HELP ME FEEL THE WAY I WANT IS:

TODAY, I INTEND TO:

I AM PRACTICING SELF-CARE TODAY BY:

Time to Check In

HOW IS YOUR DAILY GRATITUDE PRACTICE GOING?

ARE YOU STAYING CONSISTENT? IF NOT, WHAT CAN YOU DO TO HELP YOURSELF RECOMMIT?

DO YOU FEEL GOOD ABOUT THE PROGRESS YOU'RE MAKING?

WHAT ARE YOU LEARNING ABOUT YOURSELF?

HOW DO YOU FEEL ABOUT INCORPORATING DAILY SELF-CARE INTO YOUR LIFE?

WHAT DO YOU WANT MORE OF?

Stay committed and keep moving forward!

*"If you don't try,
you can't succeed."*

TODAY, I AM GRATEFUL FOR:

1.

2.

3.

TODAY, I AM THINKING ABOUT:

LIVING WITH GRATITUDE

TODAY, I AM FEELING:

AN ACTION I CAN TAKE TODAY TO HELP ME FEEL THE WAY I WANT IS:

TODAY, I INTEND TO:

I AM PRACTICING SELF-CARE TODAY BY:

"I'm moving forward. One day at a time, one step at a time. It might be hard, but I'm going to keep on keeping on."

TODAY, I AM GRATEFUL FOR:

1.

2.

3.

TODAY, I AM THINKING ABOUT:

LIVING WITH GRATITUDE

TODAY, I AM FEELING:

AN ACTION I CAN TAKE TODAY TO HELP ME FEEL THE WAY I WANT IS:

TODAY, I INTEND TO:

I AM PRACTICING SELF-CARE TODAY BY:

"I can spend my life worrying or I can decide to live each day to the fullest. My life, my choice."

TODAY, I AM GRATEFUL FOR:

1.

2.

3.

TODAY, I AM THINKING ABOUT:

LIVING WITH GRATITUDE

TODAY, I AM FEELING:

AN ACTION I CAN TAKE TODAY TO HELP ME FEEL THE WAY I WANT IS:

TODAY, I INTEND TO:

I AM PRACTICING SELF-CARE TODAY BY:

"Your future is whatever you have the courage to make it."

TODAY, I AM GRATEFUL FOR:

1.

2.

3.

TODAY, I AM THINKING ABOUT:

LIVING WITH GRATITUDE

TODAY, I AM FEELING:

AN ACTION I CAN TAKE TODAY TO HELP ME FEEL THE WAY I WANT IS:

TODAY, I INTEND TO:

I AM PRACTICING SELF-CARE TODAY BY:

"When you take the time to practice self care each day, you're showing yourself you matter."

TODAY, I AM GRATEFUL FOR:

1.

2.

3.

TODAY, I AM THINKING ABOUT:

LIVING WITH GRATITUDE

TODAY, I AM FEELING:

AN ACTION I CAN TAKE TODAY TO HELP ME FEEL THE WAY I WANT IS:

TODAY, I INTEND TO:

I AM PRACTICING SELF-CARE TODAY BY:

"Be the version of yourself you've been dreaming about, not who other people tell you to be."

TODAY, I AM GRATEFUL FOR:

1.

2.

3.

TODAY, I AM THINKING ABOUT:

LIVING WITH GRATITUDE

TODAY, I AM FEELING:

AN ACTION I CAN TAKE TODAY TO HELP ME FEEL THE WAY I WANT IS:

TODAY, I INTEND TO:

I AM PRACTICING SELF-CARE TODAY BY:

"The only person whose opinion truly matters is yours. If you think you can, you're right. If you think you can't, you're right. Tune out everyone else and tap into your soul."

TODAY, I AM GRATEFUL FOR:

1.

2.

3.

TODAY, I AM THINKING ABOUT:

LIVING WITH GRATITUDE

TODAY, I AM FEELING:

AN ACTION I CAN TAKE TODAY TO HELP ME FEEL THE WAY I WANT IS:

TODAY, I INTEND TO:

I AM PRACTICING SELF-CARE TODAY BY:

"Perfection doesn't exist. If you're striving for perfection, you're going to lose every time."

TODAY, I AM GRATEFUL FOR:

1.

2.

3.

TODAY, I AM THINKING ABOUT:

LIVING WITH GRATITUDE

TODAY, I AM FEELING:

AN ACTION I CAN TAKE TODAY TO HELP ME FEEL THE WAY I WANT IS:

TODAY, I INTEND TO:

I AM PRACTICING SELF-CARE TODAY BY:

"The hardest moments of your life are also the greatest opportunities to grow the most."

TODAY, I AM GRATEFUL FOR:

1.

2.

3.

TODAY, I AM THINKING ABOUT:

LIVING WITH GRATITUDE

TODAY, I AM FEELING:

AN ACTION I CAN TAKE TODAY TO HELP ME FEEL THE WAY I WANT IS:

TODAY, I INTEND TO:

I AM PRACTICING SELF-CARE TODAY BY:

"*Making mistakes is part of the game. If you aren't making mistakes you aren't taking enough risks.*"

TODAY, I AM GRATEFUL FOR:

1.

2.

3.

TODAY, I AM THINKING ABOUT:

LIVING WITH GRATITUDE

TODAY, I AM FEELING:

AN ACTION I CAN TAKE TODAY TO HELP ME FEEL THE WAY I WANT IS:

TODAY, I INTEND TO:

I AM PRACTICING SELF-CARE TODAY BY:

Time to Check In

HOW IS YOUR DAILY GRATITUDE PRACTICE GOING?

ARE YOU STAYING CONSISTENT? IF NOT, WHAT CAN YOU DO TO HELP YOURSELF RECOMMIT?

DO YOU FEEL GOOD ABOUT THE PROGRESS YOU'RE MAKING?

LIVING WITH GRATITUDE

WHAT ARE YOU LEARNING ABOUT YOURSELF?

HOW DO YOU FEEL ABOUT INCORPORATING DAILY SELF-CARE INTO YOUR LIFE?

WHAT DO YOU WANT MORE OF?

Stay committed and keep moving forward!

DARA KURTZ

"Life is made up of moments. It's what you do with these moments that determines everything."

TODAY, I AM GRATEFUL FOR:

1.

2.

3.

TODAY, I AM THINKING ABOUT:

LIVING WITH GRATITUDE

TODAY, I AM FEELING:

AN ACTION I CAN TAKE TODAY TO HELP ME FEEL THE WAY I WANT IS:

TODAY, I INTEND TO:

I AM PRACTICING SELF-CARE TODAY BY:

"All you have is today. Make peace with your past mistakes and stop trying to control the future."

TODAY, I AM GRATEFUL FOR:

1.

2.

3.

TODAY, I AM THINKING ABOUT:

LIVING WITH GRATITUDE

TODAY, I AM FEELING:

AN ACTION I CAN TAKE TODAY TO HELP ME FEEL THE WAY I WANT IS:

TODAY, I INTEND TO:

I AM PRACTICING SELF-CARE TODAY BY:

"Happiness is your human right. Be intentional about achieving it."

TODAY, I AM GRATEFUL FOR:

1.

2.

3.

TODAY, I AM THINKING ABOUT:

LIVING WITH GRATITUDE

TODAY, I AM FEELING:

AN ACTION I CAN TAKE TODAY TO HELP ME FEEL THE WAY I WANT IS:

TODAY, I INTEND TO:

I AM PRACTICING SELF-CARE TODAY BY:

"Figure out who your people are, then figure out how to spend time with them."

TODAY, I AM GRATEFUL FOR:

1.

2.

3.

TODAY, I AM THINKING ABOUT:

LIVING WITH GRATITUDE

TODAY, I AM FEELING:

AN ACTION I CAN TAKE TODAY TO HELP ME FEEL THE WAY I WANT IS:

TODAY, I INTEND TO:

I AM PRACTICING SELF-CARE TODAY BY:

> *"A peaceful mind creates a peaceful body."*

TODAY, I AM GRATEFUL FOR:

1.

2.

3.

TODAY, I AM THINKING ABOUT:

LIVING WITH GRATITUDE

TODAY, I AM FEELING:

AN ACTION I CAN TAKE TODAY TO HELP ME FEEL THE WAY I WANT IS:

TODAY, I INTEND TO:

I AM PRACTICING SELF-CARE TODAY BY:

*"Your daily habits can get you where you
want to go—or hold you back."*

TODAY, I AM GRATEFUL FOR:

1.

2.

3.

TODAY, I AM THINKING ABOUT:

LIVING WITH GRATITUDE

TODAY, I AM FEELING:

AN ACTION I CAN TAKE TODAY TO HELP ME FEEL THE WAY I WANT IS:

TODAY, I INTEND TO:

I AM PRACTICING SELF-CARE TODAY BY:

"Happiness is a choice we make for ourselves every day."

TODAY, I AM GRATEFUL FOR:

1.

2.

3.

TODAY, I AM THINKING ABOUT:

LIVING WITH GRATITUDE

TODAY, I AM FEELING:

AN ACTION I CAN TAKE TODAY TO HELP ME FEEL THE WAY I WANT IS:

TODAY, I INTEND TO:

I AM PRACTICING SELF-CARE TODAY BY:

DARA KURTZ

"Being content with your life and the choices you've made is a gift no one can take from you."

TODAY, I AM GRATEFUL FOR:

1.

2.

3.

TODAY, I AM THINKING ABOUT:

LIVING WITH GRATITUDE

TODAY, I AM FEELING:

AN ACTION I CAN TAKE TODAY TO HELP ME FEEL THE WAY I WANT IS:

TODAY, I INTEND TO:

I AM PRACTICING SELF-CARE TODAY BY:

"If you don't make yourself a priority, don't expect anyone else to either."

TODAY, I AM GRATEFUL FOR:

1.

2.

3.

TODAY, I AM THINKING ABOUT:

TODAY, I AM FEELING:

AN ACTION I CAN TAKE TODAY TO HELP ME FEEL THE WAY I WANT IS:

TODAY, I INTEND TO:

I AM PRACTICING SELF-CARE TODAY BY:

"A grateful heart creates a joyful soul."

TODAY, I AM GRATEFUL FOR:

1.

2.

3.

TODAY, I AM THINKING ABOUT:

LIVING WITH GRATITUDE

TODAY, I AM FEELING:

AN ACTION I CAN TAKE TODAY TO HELP ME FEEL THE WAY I WANT IS:

TODAY, I INTEND TO:

I AM PRACTICING SELF-CARE TODAY BY:

Time to Check In

HOW IS YOUR DAILY GRATITUDE PRACTICE GOING?

ARE YOU STAYING CONSISTENT? IF NOT, WHAT CAN YOU DO TO HELP YOURSELF RECOMMIT?

DO YOU FEEL GOOD ABOUT THE PROGRESS YOU'RE MAKING?

WHAT ARE YOU LEARNING ABOUT YOURSELF?

HOW DO YOU FEEL ABOUT INCORPORATING DAILY SELF-CARE INTO YOUR LIFE?

WHAT DO YOU WANT MORE OF?

Stay committed and keep moving forward!

"Wake up and notice the blessings in your life every day. If you can't see them, keep looking. They're there."

TODAY, I AM GRATEFUL FOR:

1.

2.

3.

TODAY, I AM THINKING ABOUT:

LIVING WITH GRATITUDE

TODAY, I AM FEELING:

AN ACTION I CAN TAKE TODAY TO HELP ME FEEL THE WAY I WANT IS:

TODAY, I INTEND TO:

I AM PRACTICING SELF-CARE TODAY BY:

"Get comfortable spending time alone. When you learn to be your own best friend, magical things can happen."

TODAY, I AM GRATEFUL FOR:

1.

2.

3.

TODAY, I AM THINKING ABOUT:

LIVING WITH GRATITUDE

TODAY, I AM FEELING:

AN ACTION I CAN TAKE TODAY TO HELP ME FEEL THE WAY I WANT IS:

TODAY, I INTEND TO:

I AM PRACTICING SELF-CARE TODAY BY:

"Creating a meaningful life takes work, but it's one of the most important jobs of your life."

TODAY, I AM GRATEFUL FOR:

1.

2.

3.

TODAY, I AM THINKING ABOUT:

LIVING WITH GRATITUDE

TODAY, I AM FEELING:

AN ACTION I CAN TAKE TODAY TO HELP ME FEEL THE WAY I WANT IS:

TODAY, I INTEND TO:

I AM PRACTICING SELF-CARE TODAY BY:

"Stop listening to other people; listen to the voice inside yourself."

TODAY, I AM GRATEFUL FOR:

1.

2.

3.

TODAY, I AM THINKING ABOUT:

LIVING WITH GRATITUDE

TODAY, I AM FEELING:

AN ACTION I CAN TAKE TODAY TO HELP ME FEEL THE WAY I WANT IS:

TODAY, I INTEND TO:

I AM PRACTICING SELF-CARE TODAY BY:

> *"You will never figure out the answers if you never ask the questions."*

TODAY, I AM GRATEFUL FOR:

1.

2.

3.

TODAY, I AM THINKING ABOUT:

LIVING WITH GRATITUDE

TODAY, I AM FEELING:

AN ACTION I CAN TAKE TODAY TO HELP ME FEEL THE WAY I WANT IS:

TODAY, I INTEND TO:

I AM PRACTICING SELF-CARE TODAY BY:

"Failure is part of life. When something doesn't go the way you want, learn from it and try again."

TODAY, I AM GRATEFUL FOR:

1.

2.

3.

TODAY, I AM THINKING ABOUT:

LIVING WITH GRATITUDE

TODAY, I AM FEELING:

AN ACTION I CAN TAKE TODAY TO HELP ME FEEL THE WAY I WANT IS:

TODAY, I INTEND TO:

I AM PRACTICING SELF-CARE TODAY BY:

> *"You don't have to have everything figured out. Just start, and the rest will follow."*

TODAY, I AM GRATEFUL FOR:

1.

2.

3.

TODAY, I AM THINKING ABOUT:

LIVING WITH GRATITUDE

TODAY, I AM FEELING:

AN ACTION I CAN TAKE TODAY TO HELP ME FEEL THE WAY I WANT IS:

TODAY, I INTEND TO:

I AM PRACTICING SELF-CARE TODAY BY:

"Getting to know yourself is the greatest gift."

TODAY, I AM GRATEFUL FOR:

1.

2.

3.

TODAY, I AM THINKING ABOUT:

LIVING WITH GRATITUDE

TODAY, I AM FEELING:

AN ACTION I CAN TAKE TODAY TO HELP ME FEEL THE WAY I WANT IS:

TODAY, I INTEND TO:

I AM PRACTICING SELF-CARE TODAY BY:

> *"Trust the Universe is on your side and that all you want is on its way to you."*

TODAY, I AM GRATEFUL FOR:

1.

2.

3.

TODAY, I AM THINKING ABOUT:

LIVING WITH GRATITUDE

TODAY, I AM FEELING:

AN ACTION I CAN TAKE TODAY TO HELP ME FEEL THE WAY I WANT IS:

TODAY, I INTEND TO:

I AM PRACTICING SELF-CARE TODAY BY:

"Counting your blessings is the secret to a happy life."

TODAY, I AM GRATEFUL FOR:

1.

2.

3.

TODAY, I AM THINKING ABOUT:

LIVING WITH GRATITUDE

TODAY, I AM FEELING:

AN ACTION I CAN TAKE TODAY TO HELP ME FEEL THE WAY I WANT IS:

TODAY, I INTEND TO:

I AM PRACTICING SELF-CARE TODAY BY:

Time to Check In

HOW IS YOUR DAILY GRATITUDE PRACTICE GOING?

ARE YOU STAYING CONSISTENT? IF NOT, WHAT CAN YOU DO TO HELP YOURSELF RECOMMIT?

DO YOU FEEL GOOD ABOUT THE PROGRESS YOU'RE MAKING?

WHAT ARE YOU LEARNING ABOUT YOURSELF?

HOW DO YOU FEEL ABOUT INCORPORATING DAILY SELF-CARE INTO YOUR LIFE?

I hope you're enjoying this journal! Don't forget to order another one soon. You don't want to miss a day of this beautiful habit you've worked so hard to build. While you're at it, order one for a friend and spread the love.

Dara

"Focus on what you have, not what you lack."

TODAY, I AM GRATEFUL FOR:

1.

2.

3.

TODAY, I AM THINKING ABOUT:

LIVING WITH GRATITUDE

TODAY, I AM FEELING:

AN ACTION I CAN TAKE TODAY TO HELP ME FEEL THE WAY I WANT IS:

TODAY, I INTEND TO:

I AM PRACTICING SELF-CARE TODAY BY:

*"If you don't try,
you can't succeed."*

TODAY, I AM GRATEFUL FOR:

1.

2.

3.

TODAY, I AM THINKING ABOUT:

LIVING WITH GRATITUDE

TODAY, I AM FEELING:

AN ACTION I CAN TAKE TODAY TO HELP ME FEEL THE WAY I WANT IS:

TODAY, I INTEND TO:

I AM PRACTICING SELF-CARE TODAY BY:

"I'm moving forward. One day at a time, one step at a time. It might be hard, but I'm going to keep on keeping on."

TODAY, I AM GRATEFUL FOR:

1.

2.

3.

TODAY, I AM THINKING ABOUT:

LIVING WITH GRATITUDE

TODAY, I AM FEELING:

AN ACTION I CAN TAKE TODAY TO HELP ME FEEL THE WAY I WANT IS:

TODAY, I INTEND TO:

I AM PRACTICING SELF-CARE TODAY BY:

DARA KURTZ

"I can spend my life worrying or I can decide to live each day to the fullest. My life, my choice."

TODAY, I AM GRATEFUL FOR:

1.

2.

3.

TODAY, I AM THINKING ABOUT:

LIVING WITH GRATITUDE

TODAY, I AM FEELING:

AN ACTION I CAN TAKE TODAY TO HELP ME FEEL THE WAY I WANT IS:

TODAY, I INTEND TO:

I AM PRACTICING SELF-CARE TODAY BY:

"Your future is whatever you have the courage to make it."

TODAY, I AM GRATEFUL FOR:

1.

2.

3.

TODAY, I AM THINKING ABOUT:

LIVING WITH GRATITUDE

TODAY, I AM FEELING:

AN ACTION I CAN TAKE TODAY TO HELP ME FEEL THE WAY I WANT IS:

TODAY, I INTEND TO:

I AM PRACTICING SELF-CARE TODAY BY:

"When you take the time to practice self care each day, you're showing yourself you matter."

TODAY, I AM GRATEFUL FOR:

1.

2.

3.

TODAY, I AM THINKING ABOUT:

LIVING WITH GRATITUDE

TODAY, I AM FEELING:

AN ACTION I CAN TAKE TODAY TO HELP ME FEEL THE WAY I WANT IS:

TODAY, I INTEND TO:

I AM PRACTICING SELF-CARE TODAY BY:

DARA KURTZ

"Be the version of yourself you've been dreaming about, not who other people tell you to be."

TODAY, I AM GRATEFUL FOR:

1.

2.

3.

TODAY, I AM THINKING ABOUT:

LIVING WITH GRATITUDE

TODAY, I AM FEELING:

AN ACTION I CAN TAKE TODAY TO HELP ME FEEL THE WAY I WANT IS:

TODAY, I INTEND TO:

I AM PRACTICING SELF-CARE TODAY BY:

"The only person whose opinion truly matters is yours. If you think you can, you're right. If you think you can't, you're right. Tune out everyone else and tap into your soul."

TODAY, I AM GRATEFUL FOR:

1.

2.

3.

TODAY, I AM THINKING ABOUT:

LIVING WITH GRATITUDE

TODAY, I AM FEELING:

AN ACTION I CAN TAKE TODAY TO HELP ME FEEL THE WAY I WANT IS:

TODAY, I INTEND TO:

I AM PRACTICING SELF-CARE TODAY BY:

Thank you for spending a little time with me each day!

I hope you're enjoying this habit and are feeling happier and more joyful. Make sure to order another journal to keep it up. You worked hard to establish this daily habit and you want to stick with it.

Check out all of my books at www.crazyperfectlife.com

Dara

Made in the USA
Middletown, DE
30 March 2023

27355023R00088